D1468156

SEP 2005

No Backbone!
The World of Invertebrates

Tricky Trapdoor Spiders

by Meish Goldish

Consultant: Brian V. Brown
Curator, Entomology Section
Natural History Museum of Los Angeles County

BEARPORT
PUBLISHING

NEW YORK, NEW YORK

Credits

Cover, © O.S.F./Animals Animals-Earth Scenes, © Hans Christoph Kappel/Minden Pictures; Title page, © Hans Christoph Kappel/Minden Pictures; 4–5, © O.S.F./Animals Animals-Earth Scenes; 6, © Dr. Paul Zahl/Photo Researchers, Inc.; 7, © Hans Christoph Kappel/Minden Pictures; 8, © Dr. Paul Zahl/Photo Researchers, Inc.; 9, © Hans Christoph Kappel/Minden Pictures; 10T, © Jacob Kalichman; 10B, © N. A. S./Photo Researchers, Inc.; 11, © Amir Ridhwan Mohd Ghazali; 12, © Blickwinkel/Hecker/Alamy; 13, © James H. Robinson/Photo Researchers, Inc.; 14T, © Mark A. Newton; 14C, © Hans Christoph Kappel/Nature Picture Library; 14B, © M. & C. Photography/Peter Arnold Inc.; 15, © Ingo Arndt/Nature Picture Library; 16, © Oxford Scientific Films/Photolibrary; 18, © Clipart.com; 19, © Peter J. Bryant/ Biological Photo Service & Terraphotographics; 20–21, © Marshal Hedin; 22TL, © John Bell/Shutterstock; 22TR, © Bryan Reynolds/Oxford Scientific/Photolibrary; 22BL, © Stephen Dalton/Minden Pictures; 22BR, © Tom Brakefield/ SuperStock; 23TL, © Jim Wehtje/Photodisc Green/Getty Images; 22TR, © Blickwinkel/Hecker/Alamy; 23BL, © Marshal Hedin; 23BR, © Hans Christoph Kappel/Minden Pictures; 24, © Jacob Kalichman.

Publisher: Kenn Goin
Editorial Director: Adam Siegel
Creative Director: Spencer Brinker
Design: Dawn Beard Creative
Photo Researcher: Beaura Kathy Ringrose

Library of Congress Cataloging-in-Publication Data

Goldish, Meish.
 Tricky trapdoor spiders / by Meish Goldish.
    p. cm. — (No backbone! The world of invertebrates)
 Includes bibliographical references and index.
 ISBN-13: 978-1-59716-707-9 (library binding)
 ISBN-10: 1-59716-707-X (library binding)
 1. Trap-door spiders—Juvenile literature. I. Title.

QL458.4.G65 2009
595.4'4—dc22
                          2008007203

For more information, write to Bearport Publishing Company, Inc., 101 Fifth Avenue, Suite 6R, New York, New York 10003. Printed in the United States of America.

10 9 8 7 6 5 4 3 2 1

Contents

Tricky Spiders

Trapdoor **spiders** are very tricky.

Many other spiders spin webs to trap insects to eat.

A trapdoor spider catches its food in a different way.

It waits in a hole in the ground, under a hidden door.

When an insect walks by, the tricky spider flips the door open, jumps out of the hole, and grabs it.

A trapdoor spider is about one inch (2.5 cm) long. It has eight legs, like all spiders.

5

Digging Deep

The deep, narrow hole where a trapdoor spider waits is called a burrow.

The spider works hard to make this underground hiding place.

First, it digs out dirt using a row of sharp points on its **fangs**.

The hole it makes can be about one foot (30 cm) deep.

Then the spider lines the walls with silk so they don't cave in.

Like all spiders, a trapdoor spider uses tiny tubes in its body to make silk threads. The tubes are called spinnerets.

burrow

burrow

7

Covering Up

A trapdoor spider covers its burrow with a round door.

The spider makes this **trapdoor** out of silk and mud.

It uses silk to attach the trapdoor to the burrow's opening.

Once the door is connected, the spider can flip it open and closed.

There are about 120 kinds of trapdoor spiders. Some kinds make doors that are light and thin. Others make thicker, heavier doors.

trapdoor

trapdoor spider
opening door

9

Waiting for Dinner

Most trapdoor spiders hunt at night.

They wait inside their burrows for insects to come by.

A trapdoor spider has eight eyes but it cannot see very well.

Instead, the hairs on its body feel the air move when an insect is walking nearby.

The spider then quickly opens the trapdoor, leaps forward, and grabs its victim.

hair

beetle

Some trapdoor spiders stretch lines of silk around their trapdoors. When an insect trips on the silk, the spider feels the movement and attacks.

trapdoor

lines of silk

Time to Eat

A trapdoor spider drags its victim into its burrow.

The spider poisons the insect by biting it with its fangs.

The spider also spits juices from its stomach onto the insect.

These juices turn the insect's insides into a liquid.

The spider sucks up the liquid until all that's left is the insect's empty shell!

fangs

Trapdoor spiders eat ants, beetles, cockroaches, crickets, and grasshoppers.

cockroach

13

Hiding from Enemies

scorpion

A burrow is a place for a trapdoor spider to hide when it is hunting.

It is also a good place for the spider to hide from scorpions, birds, mice, and other enemies.

closed trapdoor

The trapdoor makes the burrow hard to see.

If an enemy spots the door and tries to open it, the spider inside tries hard to stay safe.

It holds the door shut with its fangs and legs.

spider wasp

Some kinds of wasps can get inside a trapdoor spider's burrow. They chew through the trapdoor and attack the spider.

Warm Places, Cool Burrows

Trapdoor spiders are found all over the world.

They live in places that are warm.

Luckily, when the trapdoor is closed it blocks out the sun.

The closed door keeps the spider's home from getting too hot.

Trapdoor spiders spend most of their lives in their burrows.

Trapdoor Spiders Around the World

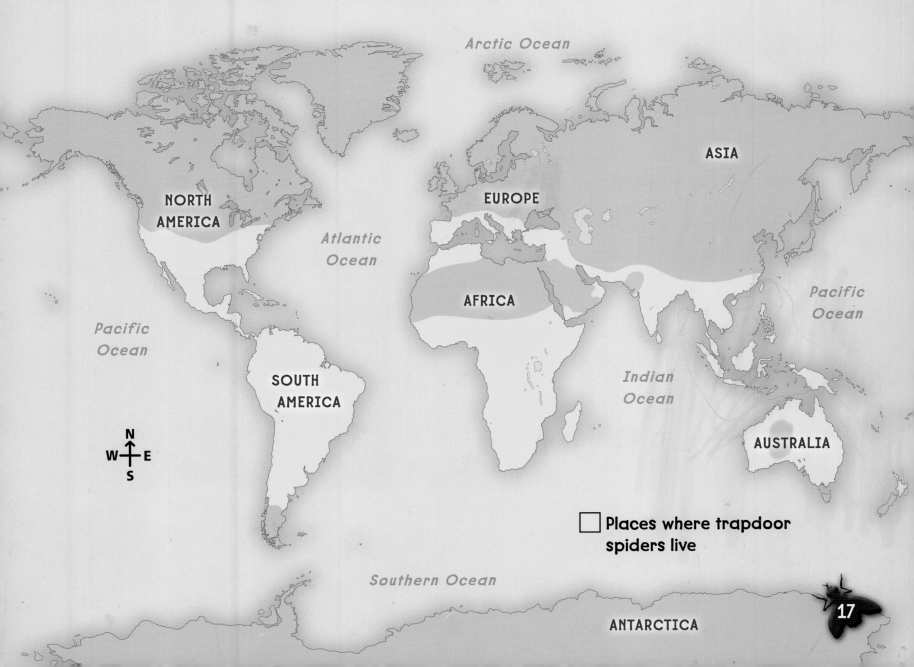

Arctic Ocean

ASIA

EUROPE

NORTH
AMERICA

Atlantic
Ocean

AFRICA

Pacific
Ocean

Pacific
Ocean

SOUTH
AMERICA

Indian
Ocean

AUSTRALIA

N
W + E
S

☐ Places where trapdoor
spiders live

Southern Ocean

ANTARCTICA

17

Little Spiders

A female trapdoor spider uses her burrow as a place to lay her eggs.

She lays about 100 eggs at a time.

The mother protects the eggs by wrapping them in a bag of silk, called an egg sac.

She attaches the egg sac to the lining of her burrow and watches over it.

After the eggs hatch, the new spiders live in the burrow for a few weeks and then go off on their own.

egg sac

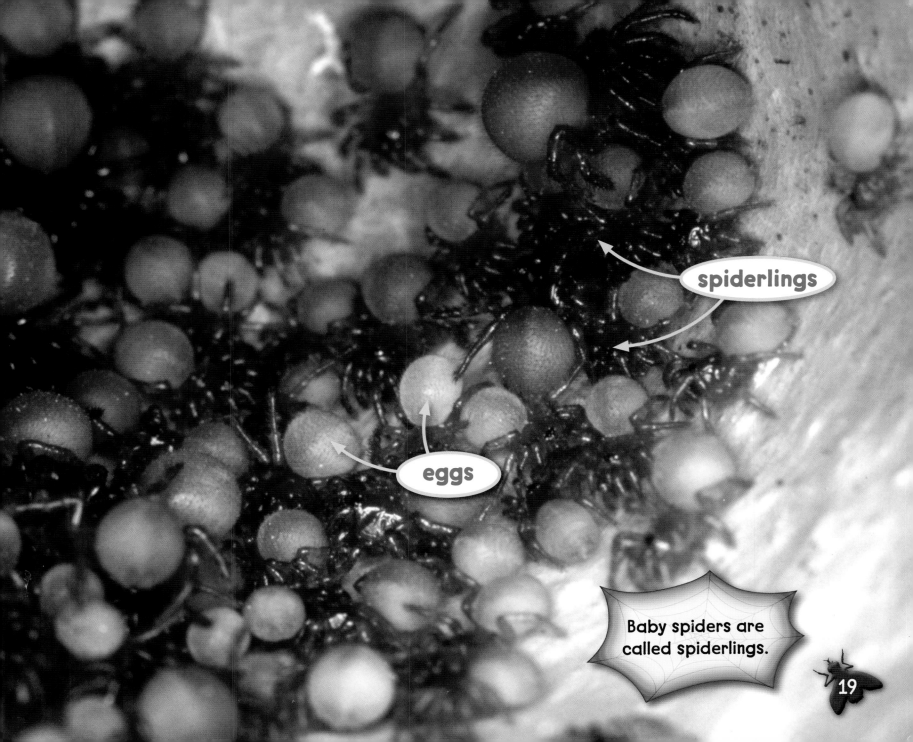

spiderlings

eggs

Baby spiders are
called spiderlings.

Growing Up

Like all spiders, trapdoor spiders have a hard covering called an exoskeleton.

As the spiders get bigger, they shed their old coverings and grow new ones.

This change is called molting.

Trapdoor spiders molt several times as they grow into adults.

Then they dig their own burrows— where they can hunt, hide from enemies, and raise new baby spiders.

Trapdoor spiders usually live about 1 or 2 years. Some females, however, can live 20 years or more.

A World of Invertebrates

An animal that has a skeleton with a **backbone** inside its body is a *vertebrate* (VUR-tuh-brit). Mammals, birds, fish, reptiles, and amphibians are all vertebrates.

An animal that does not have a skeleton with a backbone inside its body is an *invertebrate* (in-VUR-tuh-brit). More than 95 percent of all kinds of animals on Earth are invertebrates.

Some invertebrates, such as insects and spiders, have hard skeletons—called exoskeletons—on the outside of their bodies. Other invertebrates, such as worms and jellyfish, have soft, squishy bodies with no exoskeletons to protect them.

Here are four spiders that are closely related to trapdoor spiders. Like all spiders, they are invertebrates.

Mexican Redknee Tarantula

Funnel-Web Tarantula

Purseweb Spider

Baboon Spider

Glossary

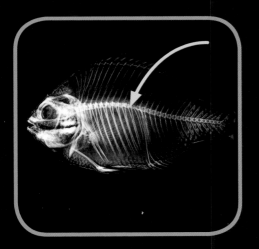

backbone
(BAK-*bohn*)
a group of connected bones that run along the backs of some animals, such as dogs, cats, and fish; also called a spine

fangs
(FANGZ)
long pointy teeth

spiders
(SPYE-durz)
small animals that have eight legs, two main body parts, and a hard covering called an exoskeleton

trapdoor
(TRAP-DOR)
a door used to hide an opening in a ceiling, floor, or roof

Index

Read More

Gerholdt, James E. *Trapdoor Spiders.* Edina, MN: ABDO & Daughters (1996).

Martin, Louise. *Trapdoor Spiders.* Vero Beach, FL: Rourke Enterprises (1988).

Learn More Online

To learn more about trapdoor spiders, visit
www.bearportpublishing.com/NoBackbone-Spiders

About the Author

Meish Goldish has written more than 100 books for children. He lives in Brooklyn, New York, in a home with no trapdoors.